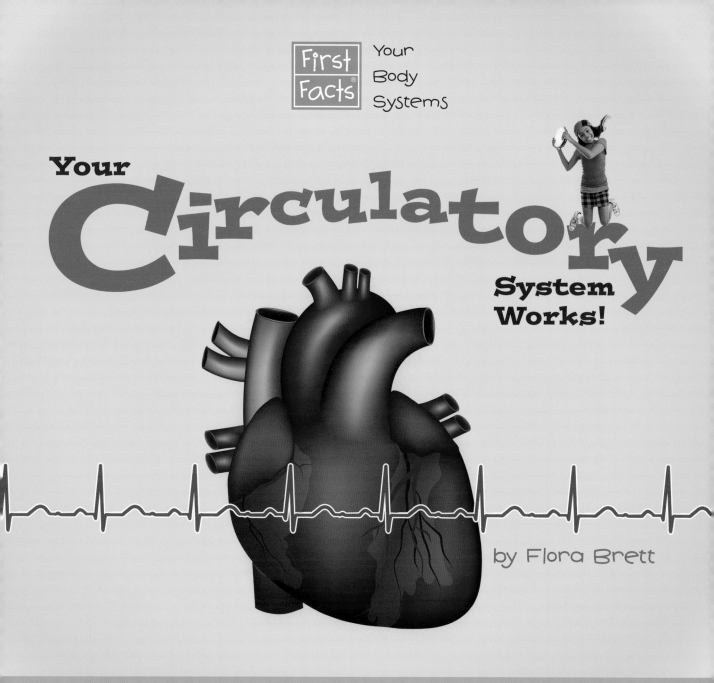

First Facts® Your Body Systems

Your Circulatory System Works!

by Flora Brett

CAPSTONE PRESS
a capstone imprint

First Facts are published by Capstone Press,
1710 Roe Crest Drive, North Mankato, Minnesota 56003
www.capstonepub.com

Library of Congress Cataloging-in-Publication Data
Brett, Flora, author.
Your circulatory system works! / by Flora Brett.
    pages cm. — (First facts. Your body systems)
Summary: "Engaging text and informative images help readers learn about their circulatory
system."— Provided by publisher.
Audience: Ages 6–9.
Audience: K to grade 3.
Includes bibliographical references and index.
ISBN 978-1-4914-2063-8 (library binding) — ISBN 978-1-4914-2247-2 (pbk.) —
ISBN 978-1-4914-2269-4 (ebook PDF)
1. Cardiovascular system—Juvenile literature. 2. Heart—Juvenile literature. 3. Blood—Juvenile
literature. 4. Human physiology—Juvenile literature. [1. Circulatory system.] I. Title.
QM178.B74 2015
612.1—dc23   2014023828

Editorial Credits
Emily Raij and Nikki Bruno Clapper, editors; Cynthia Akiyoshi, designer;
Svetlana Zhurkin, media researcher; Laura Manthe, production specialist

Photo Credits
Shutterstock: Alila Medical Media, 15, AntiMartina (dotted background), cover and throughout,
bikeriderlondon, 17, BioMedical, 19, Derek Latta, cover (top right), back cover, 1 (top right),
Ekaterina Shilova, 11, Felix Mioznikov, 5, GRei, 1, 21, Jacek Chabraszewski, 20, Leonello
Calvetti, 9, Rob Marmion, 13, sciencepics, 7, Sebastian Kaulitzki, cover

Printed in the United States of America in North Mankato, Minnesota.
092014   008482CGS15

Table of Contents

Small Heart, Big Job

Your heart is about the size of a fist. But this small muscle does a big job! It pumps blood around your entire body to keep you alive.

Circulation is the movement of blood around the body. In about 60 seconds, your heart pumps blood to every **cell**. Your circulatory system includes your heart, blood, and **blood vessels**.

circulation—movement around many different places

cell—a tiny structure that makes up all living things

blood vessel—a tube that carries blood through your body; arteries, veins, and capillaries are blood vessels

Fact:
Laughing can relax the lining of blood vessel walls and increase blood flow. That's good for your heart and for you!

Blood and Waste

People need healthy cells to survive. In turn, cells need oxygen. Oxygen in the blood flows through blood vessels. Blood vessels carry oxygen to cells.

Cells use oxygen and make waste. One type of waste is a gas called **carbon dioxide**. Blood carries waste to the lungs and the kidneys. Then the lungs and kidneys push the waste out of your body.

Fact:
The human body can survive with one kidney instead of two.

carbon dioxide—a colorless, odorless gas that people and animals breathe out

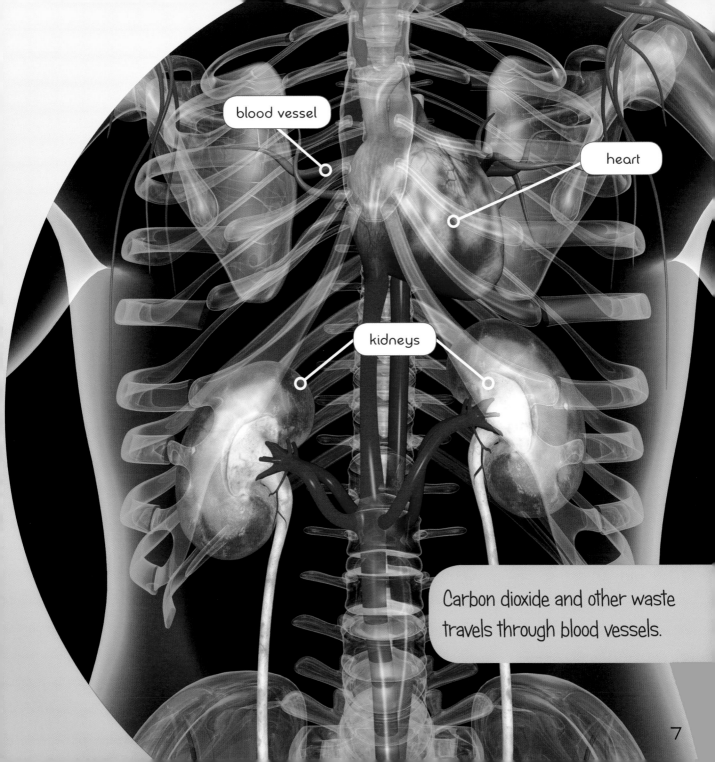

blood vessel

heart

kidneys

Carbon dioxide and other waste travels through blood vessels.

Parts of the Circulatory System

Your pumping heart and your blood vessels work together to move blood. Blood moves through branching blood vessels called arteries, veins, and capillaries.

Veins bring blood to the heart. Arteries carry blood away from the heart. Capillaries connect to arteries and veins. They carry blood to the smallest parts of the body.

Fact:

Imagine tying your blood vessels end to end. They could wrap around planet Earth more than two times!

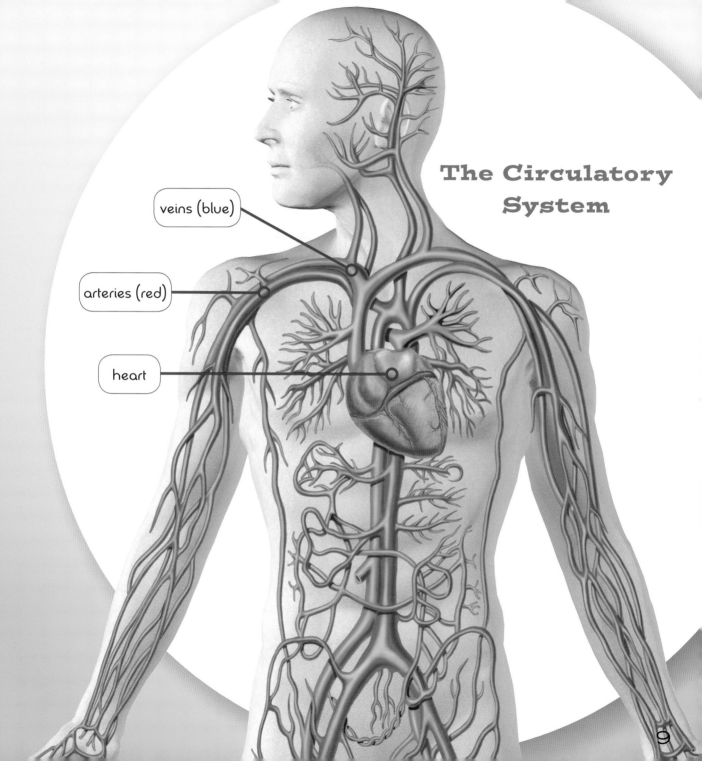

veins (blue)

arteries (red)

heart

The Circulatory System

Parts of Blood

Your blood is mostly made of water. So, what makes blood red? Red and white blood cells also float around in the blood. Red blood cells contain **hemoglobin**. Hemoglobin carries oxygen and gives blood its red color. White blood cells help your body fight infection.

Blood also contains **platelets**. When you get a cut, platelets stop the bleeding. They clump together to plug a cut blood vessel.

hemoglobin—a substance in red blood cells that carries oxygen and gives blood its red color

platelet—a tiny, flat body in the blood that helps the blood clot

Most white blood cells are made inside your bones. The cells come from a soft material called bone marrow.

red and white blood cells flowing in an artery

11

Your Amazing Heart

Your heart is the only muscle in your body that doesn't need rest. This **involuntary** muscle works all day and night. You don't even have to think about it.

Doctors listen to your heartbeat to learn how your heart is working. During normal activity, the heart beats about 70 times a minute. It beats faster when you exercise. It has to work harder.

involuntary—done without a person's control

Fact:

The heart can beat after being removed from the body. But it still needs oxygen.

How the Heart Works

The heart has four parts, or chambers. Blood flows through the top two chambers, or **atria**. Then blood enters the lower chambers, or **ventricles**. The left ventricle pumps fresh blood to the rest of the body. The right ventricle receives returning blood from veins. Then it sends blood to the lungs for more oxygen.

Blood flows between chambers through flaps called valves. Your heartbeat is the sound of the valves closing.

atrium—one of the chambers in the top of the heart that receives blood from veins

ventricle—one of the chambers in the bottom of the heart that pumps blood out to the body

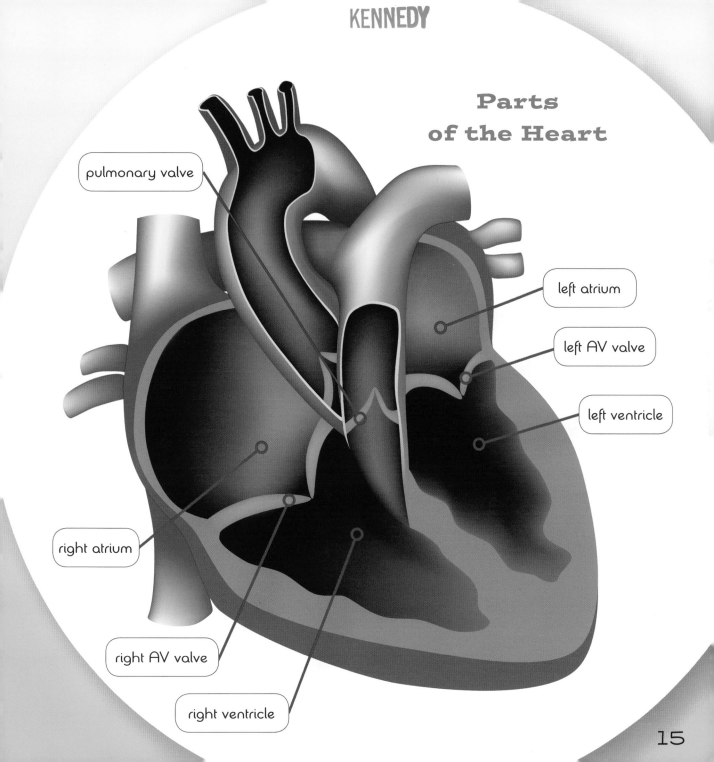

Parts of the Heart

pulmonary valve

left atrium

left AV valve

left ventricle

right atrium

right AV valve

right ventricle

Calcium from Blood to Bones

Your bones, heart, muscles, and nerves need calcium to work properly. Your blood circulates calcium throughout your body.

When you drink milk, it travels to your small intestine. Your blood then picks up the calcium in the milk.

Blood carries new calcium to your bones. Your bones also store calcium. If you don't get enough calcium from food, your blood takes calcium from your bones.

Fact:
You can get calcium from dairy products, eggs, fish, green vegetables, and fruit.

Circulatory Problems

Sometimes blood vessels get clogged with fat. It's harder for blood to travel through clogged vessels. If blood vessels clog completely, blood cannot flow through.

A heart attack happens when the heart does not get enough blood. Clogged arteries and blood **clots** can cause heart attacks. Clots stop blood from flowing back to the heart.

clot—blood that has become thicker and more solid

Fact:
A clogged artery is very difficult to unclog. People need surgery to fix this circulatory problem.

A clot (middle) stops blood (right) from flowing through an artery.

Keeping Your Heart Healthy

Eat fruits, vegetables, and other foods low in fat and high in vitamins. These healthy foods will keep your arteries free from clogs. Protect your heart by never smoking. Smoking damages your heart and blood vessels.

Fact:

Exercising for at least 30 minutes each day is great for your heart.

Amazing but True!

The heart is the body's hardest-working muscle. It even works while you're asleep! Did you know your heart also creates and sends electric signals? These signals tell the heart when to pump and how fast.

Glossary

atrium (AY-tree-uhm)—one of the chambers in the top of the heart that receives blood from veins

blood vessel (BLUHD VESS-uhl)—a tube that carries blood through your body; arteries, veins, and capillaries are blood vessels

carbon dioxide (CAR-buhn dye-AHK-syed)—a colorless, odorless gas that people and animals breathe out

cell (SEL)—a tiny structure that makes up all living things

circulation (sur-kyuh-LAY-shuhn)—movement around many different places

clot (KLOT)—blood that has become thicker and more solid

hemoglobin (HEE-muh-gloh-bin)—a substance in red blood cells that carries oxygen and gives blood its red color

involuntary (in-VOL-uhn-ter-ee)—done without a person's control

platelet (PLATE-lit)—a tiny, flat body in the blood that helps the blood clot

ventricle (VEN-tri-kuhl)—one of the chambers in the bottom of the heart that pumps blood out to the body

Read More

Ballen, Karen Gunnison. *A Tour of Your Circulatory System*. First Graphics: Body Systems. North Mankato, Minn.: Capstone Press, 2013.

Corcoran, Mary K. *The Circulatory Story*. Watertown, Mass.: Charlesbridge, 2010.

Tieck, Sarah. *Circulatory System*. Body Systems. Edina, Minn.: ABDO Pub., 2011.

Internet Sites

FactHound offers a safe, fun way to find Internet sites related to this book. All of the sites on FactHound have been researched by our staff.

Here's all you do:
Visit *www.facthound.com*
Type in this code: 9781491420638

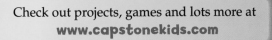

Super-cool stuff!

Check out projects, games and lots more at
www.capstonekids.com

Critical Thinking Using the Common Core

1. Different blood vessels have different jobs. Name the three blood vessel types, and explain what each one does. (Key Ideas and Details)

2. Does your heart ever beat faster while you exercise? How can you strengthen your heart and keep it healthy? (Integration of Knowledge and Ideas)

3. Explain how blood flows through your heart and to the rest of your body. (Key Ideas and Details)

Index